C.2

My Favorite Dogs

YORKSHIRE TERRIER

Jinny Johnson

A+

Smart Apple Media

Published by Smart Apple Media
P.O. Box 1329
Mankato, MN 56002

Printed in the United States of America,
at Corporate Graphics in North Mankato, Minnesota.

Designed by Hel James
Edited by Mary-Jane Wilkins

Library of Congress Cataloging-in-Publication Data

Johnson, Jinny, 1949-
 Yorkshire terrier / by Jinny Johnson.
    p. cm. -- (My favorite dog)
 Includes index.
 Summary: "Describes the care, training, and rearing of the Yorkshire
terrier. Also explains the Yorkshire terrier's unique characteristics and
history"--Provided by publisher.
 ISBN 978-1-59920-846-6 (hardcover : library bound)
 1. Yorkshire terrier--Juvenile literature. I. Title.
 SF429.Y6J64 2013
 636.76--dc23
                              2012012147

Photo acknowledgements
page 1 iStockphoto/Thinkstock; 3 Hemera/Thinkstock;
4 Cherry-Merry/Shutterstock; 5 michael d skelton/Shutterstock;
8-9 Eric Isselée/Shutterstock; 11 Nata Sdobnikova/Shutterstock;
12 iStockphoto/Thinkstock; 13 Konstantin Gushcha/Shutterstock;
14 dien/Shutterstock; 15 iStockphoto/Thinkstock; 16 Scorpp/
Shutterstock; 17 Konstantin Gushcha/Shutterstock; 18 iStockphoto/
Thinkstock; 19 cynoclub/Shutterstock; 20 & 21 Scorpp/Shutterstock;
22 iStockphoto/Thinkstock; 23 Dean Golja/Thinkstock
Cover iStockphoto/Thinkstock

DAD0504
042012
9 8 7 6 5 4 3 2 1

Contents

I'm a Yorkshire Terrier!

I may be tiny, but I'm still a terrier, and I can be brave and bold.

I'm bouncy, energetic, and cuddly too. I love to sit on my owner's lap.

What I Need

I don't need long walks, but I do like to get out every day. I love running around indoors, too, and playing games.

I like lots of company, and I get miserable if I'm left alone for long.

Don't leave
me outdoors
either.

The Yorkshire Terrier

Tail sometimes docked (shortened) to half natural length

Color: black and gold or tan, or steel-blue with gold or tan

Height: up to 9 inches (23 cm)
Weight: up to 7 pounds (3 kg)

Small, neat body

Fairly short, straight legs

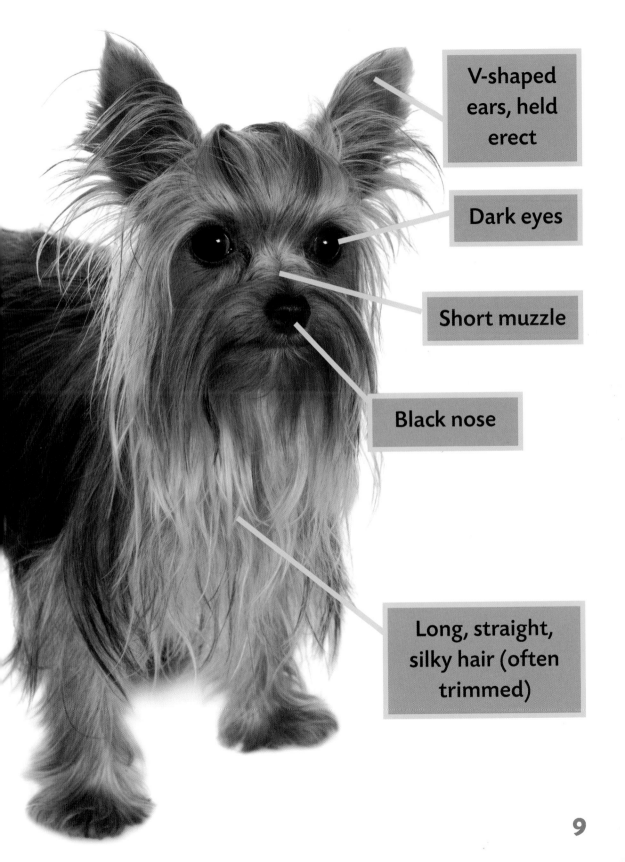

V-shaped ears, held erect

Dark eyes

Short muzzle

Black nose

Long, straight, silky hair (often trimmed)

9

All About Yorkshire Terriers

The first Yorkshire terriers (often called Yorkies) were bred in England more than 150 years ago. They worked as rat catchers in factories.

Now these little terriers are probably the second most popular breed of dog in the world. They look cute, but they are still terriers, and will bark at much larger dogs.

Growing Up

Yorkshire terrier pups need to be with their mom until they are about eight weeks old.

Yorkie puppies are born black and tan, and change color as they grow up.

All pups need careful handling, but Yorkie pups are really tiny and easily hurt. Be extra gentle, and give your puppy lots of love and attention while she gets used to her new home.

Show Dogs

Most Yorkie owners trim their pet's long hair to make it easier for the dog to run around. A trimmed Yorkie is easier to look after, too.

If you want to enter your Yorkie in dog shows, she must have long, untrimmed hair, and she will need lots of brushing and combing.

Some owners trim the hair on the dog's sides but leave a long top knot, which can be tied up in a bow.

Training your Dog

Yorkies are very intelligent little dogs and quick to learn.

They are easy to train, but they need to be shown who is boss.

A Yorkie's owner has to be the pack leader. A badly-trained Yorkie can become aggressive and snappy.

Small Dog, Big Bark

A Yorkshire terrier has a big personality in a small body. Although she is so small, a Yorkie can be a good guard dog. She likes to defend her family, and will bark and bark if a stranger comes near.

Yorkies are good with older children, but they can be nervous of young children and may snap.

It's important for everyone in the family to handle the dog properly and not to tease.

19

Your Healthy Yorkshire Terrier

Brush your Yorkie several times a week to keep her hair in good condition and remove any tangles.

Her coat will need trimming regularly unless she is a show dog.

Yorkies can have tooth problems, so brush your dog's teeth every day and take her to the vet for checkups. Her little bones can

break easily so make sure everyone handles her really gently.

Caring For Your Dog

You and your family must think very carefully before buying a Yorkshire terrier. Remember, she may live as long as 15 years.

Every day your dog must have food, water, and exercise, as well as lots of love and care.

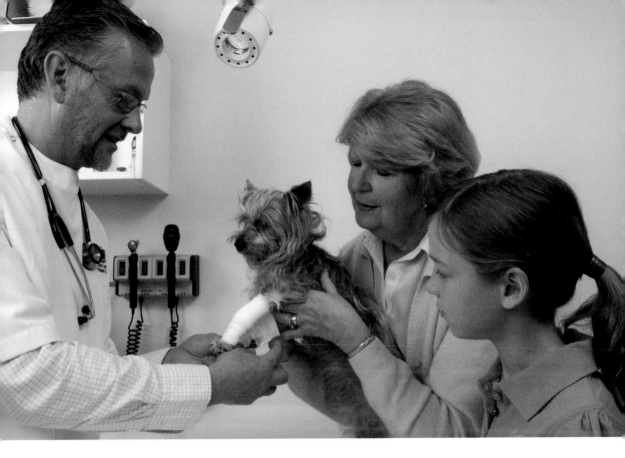

She will also need to go to the vet
for regular checks and vaccinations.
When you and your family go out,
or away on vacation, you will have
to make plans for your dog to be
looked after.

Useful Words

aggressive
An aggressive animal is likely to get into fights and attack others.

breed
A particular type of dog.

vaccination
An injection that can help protect your dog from illness.

Index